Your Beautiful Escape

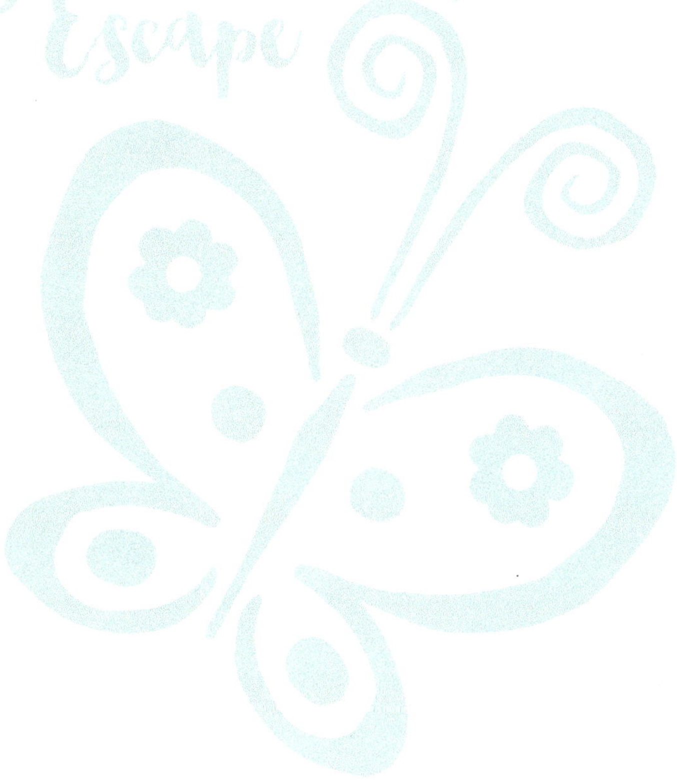

journal to self discovery

belongs to...

www.annettebridges.com

ISBN: 978-0-998157-60-3

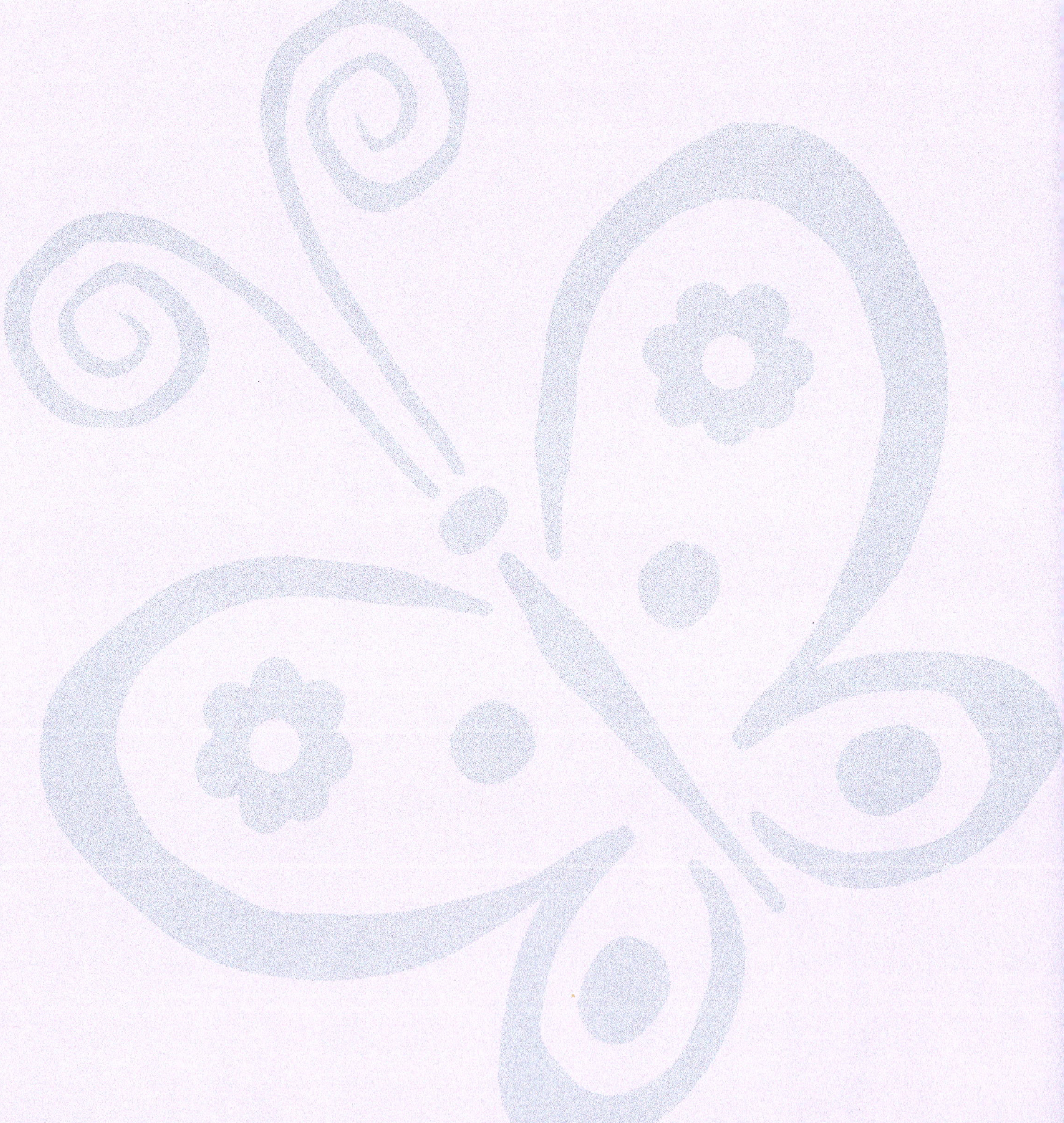

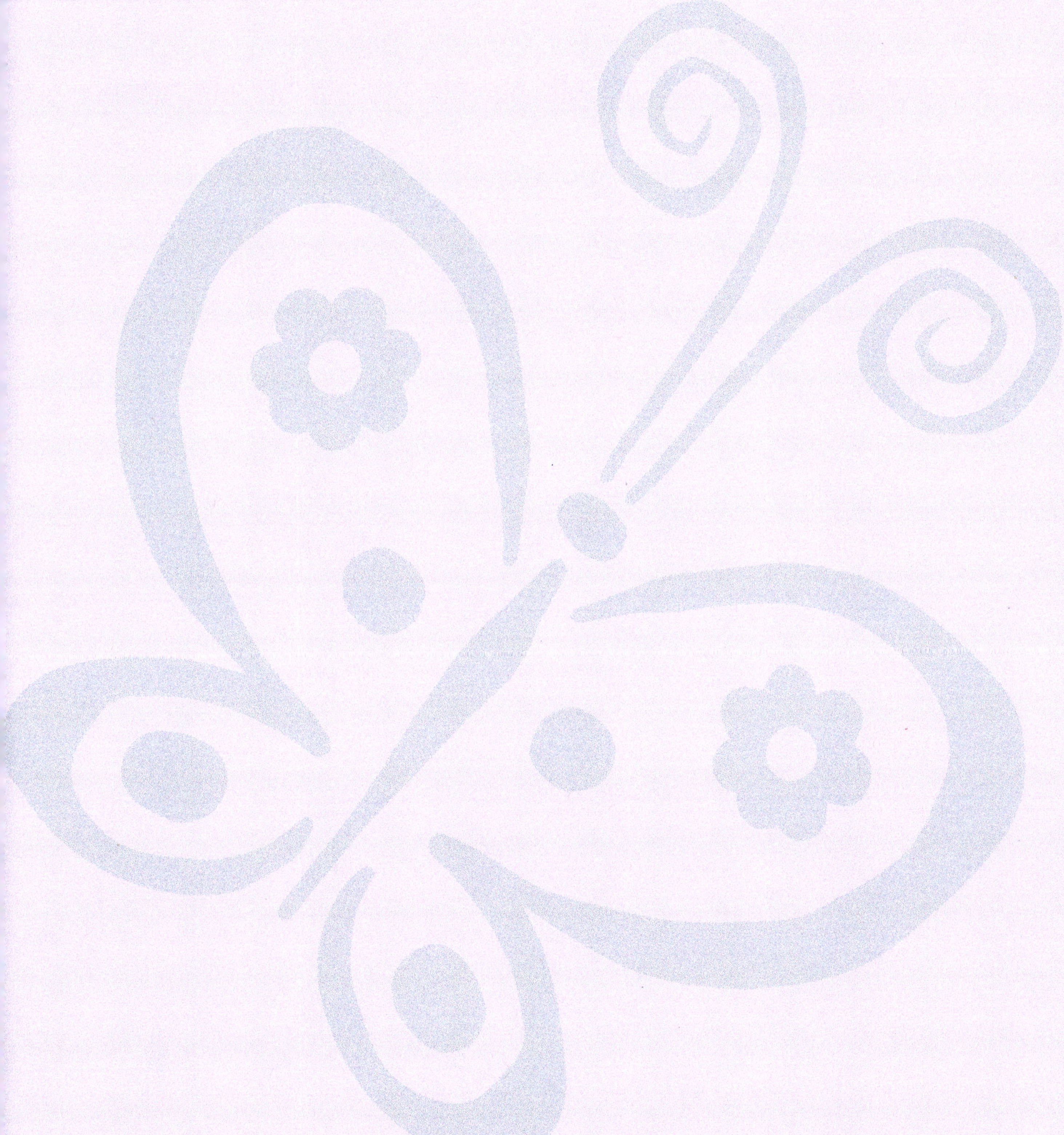

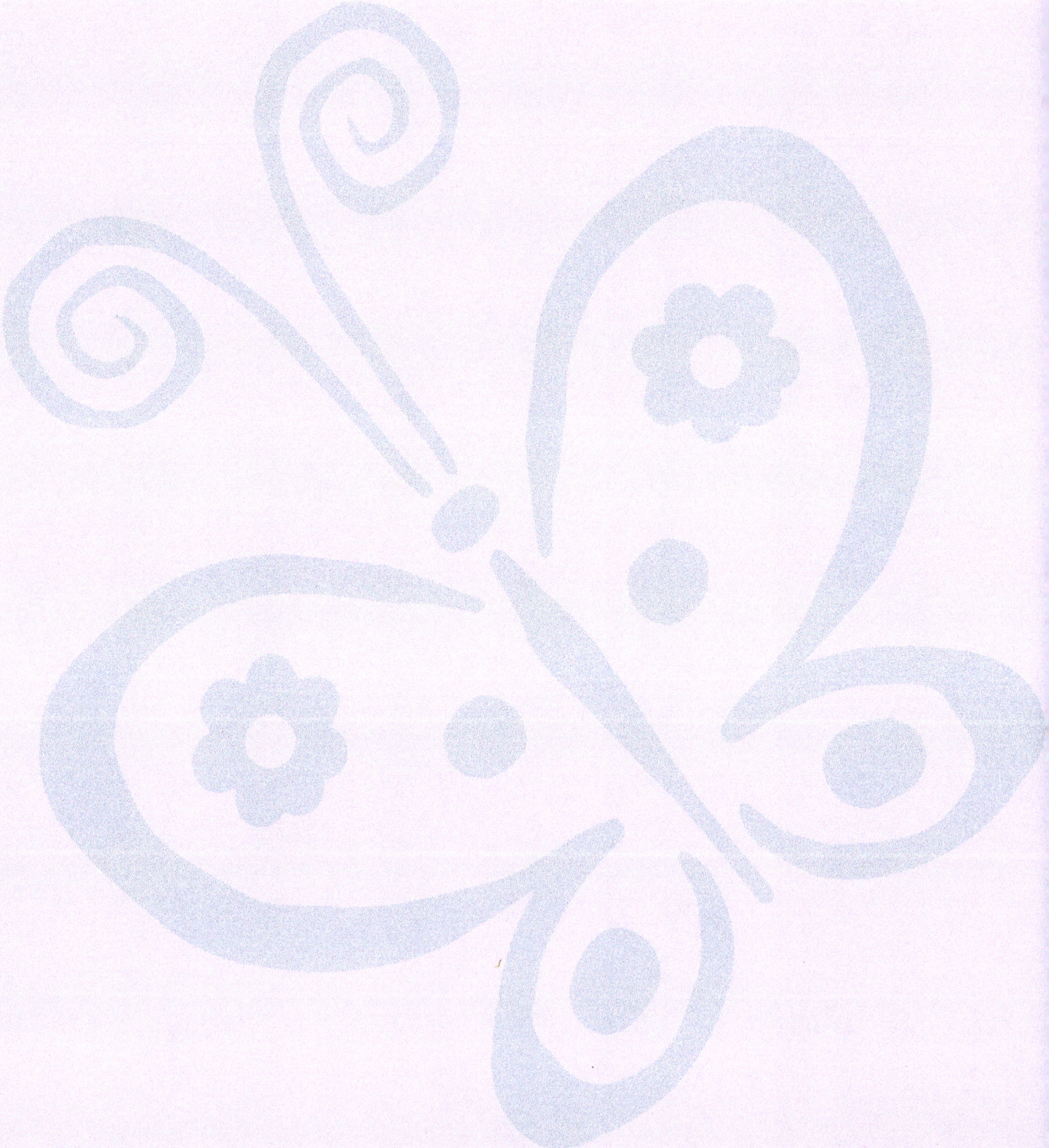

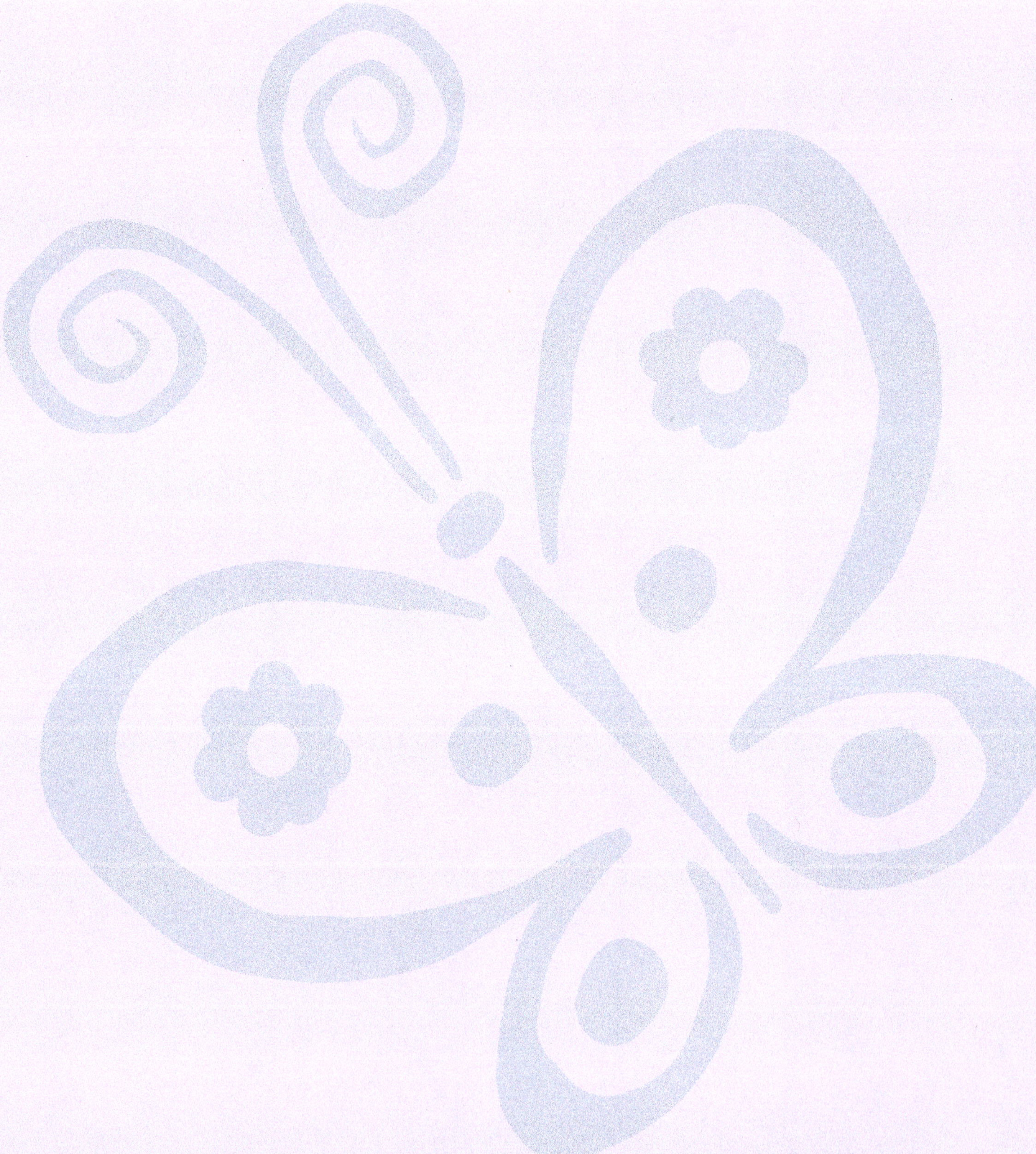

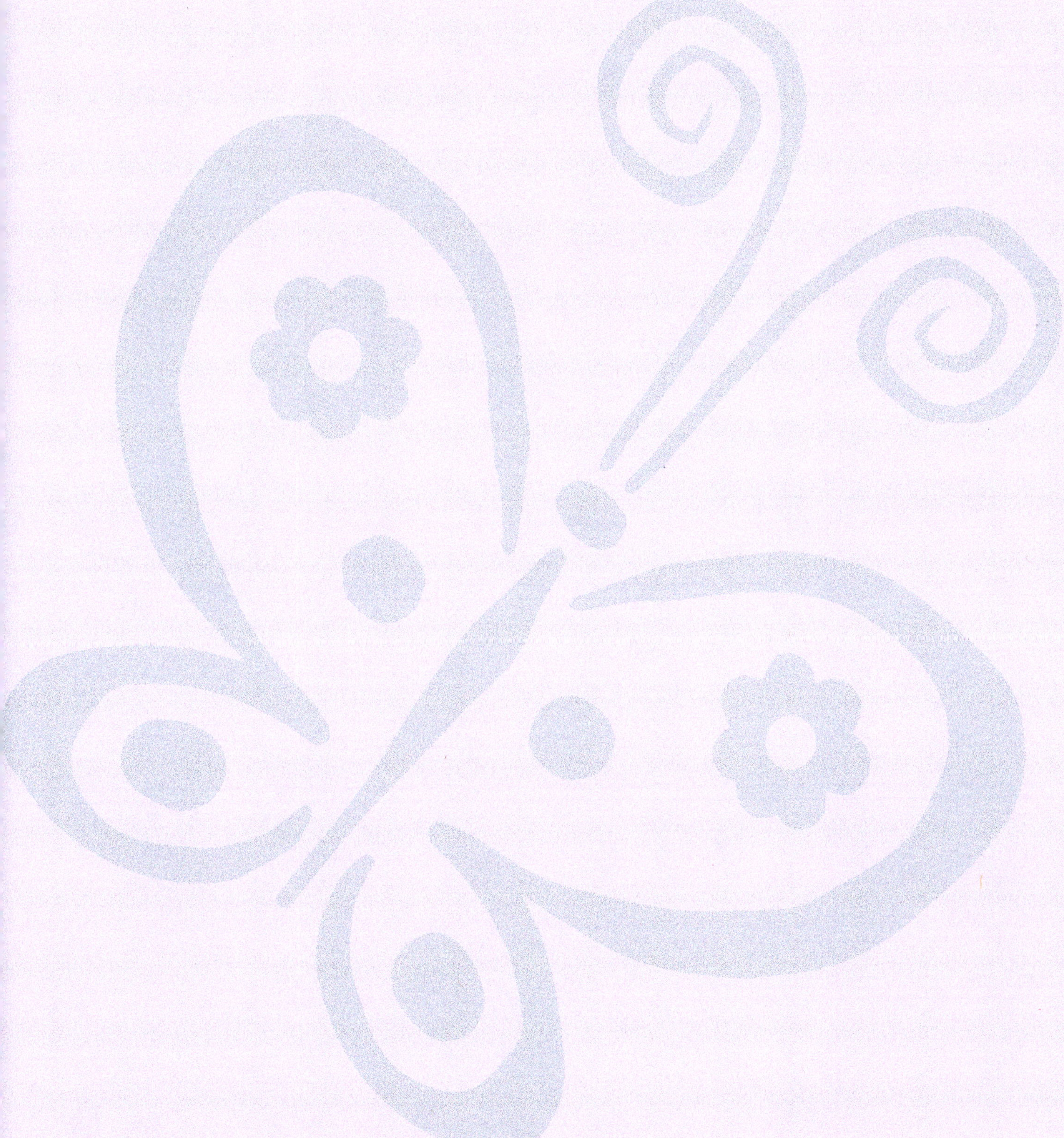

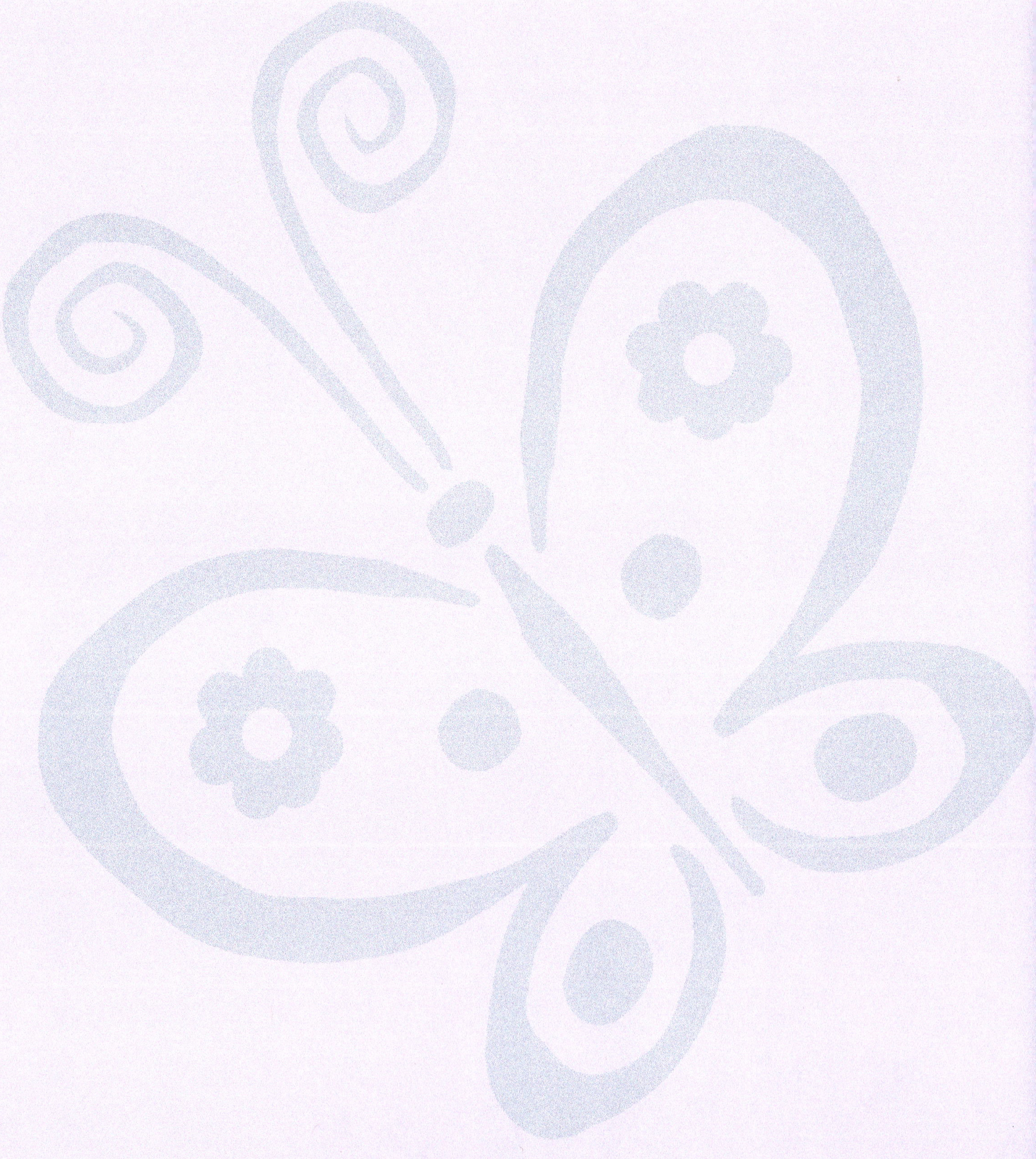

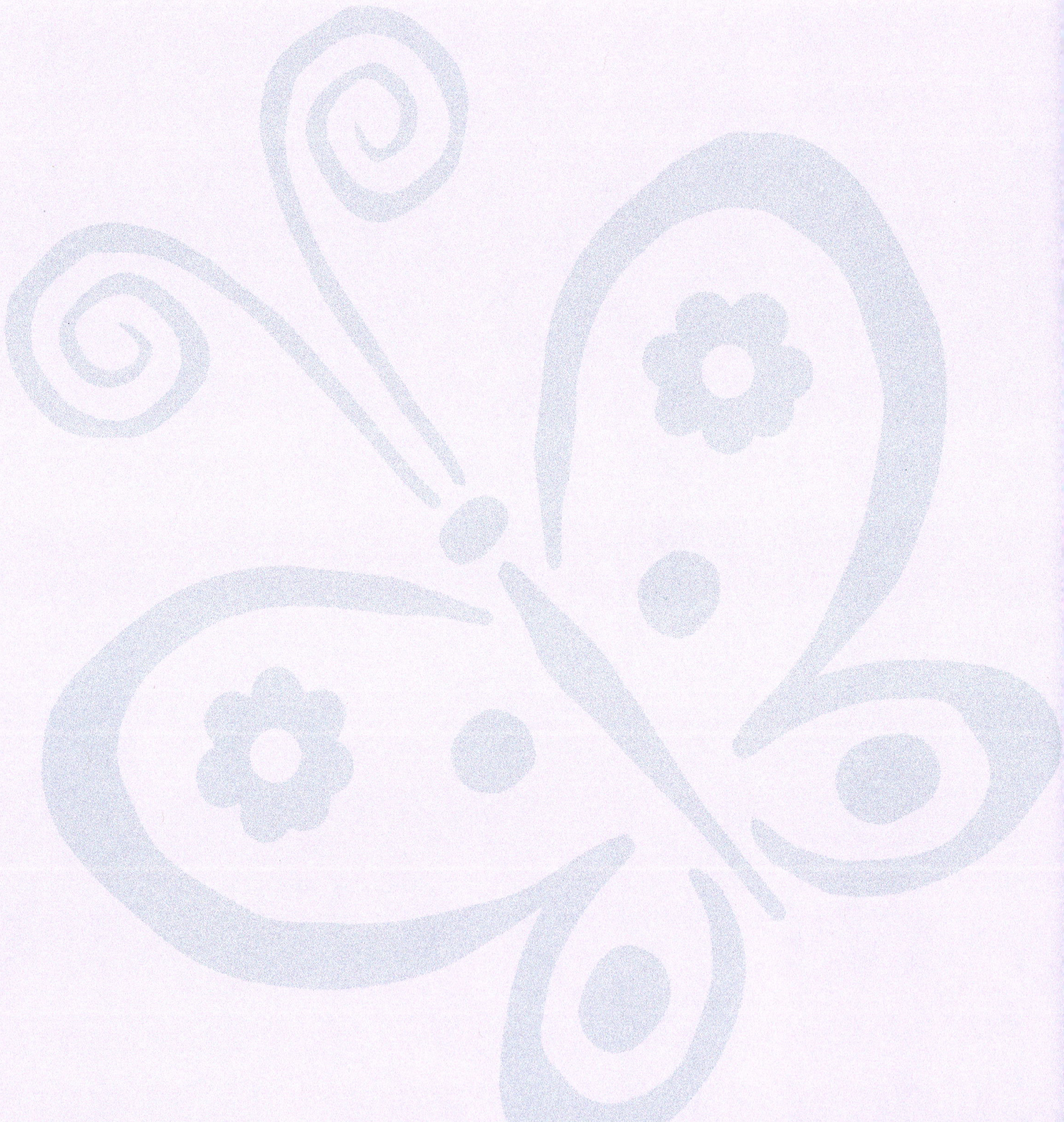

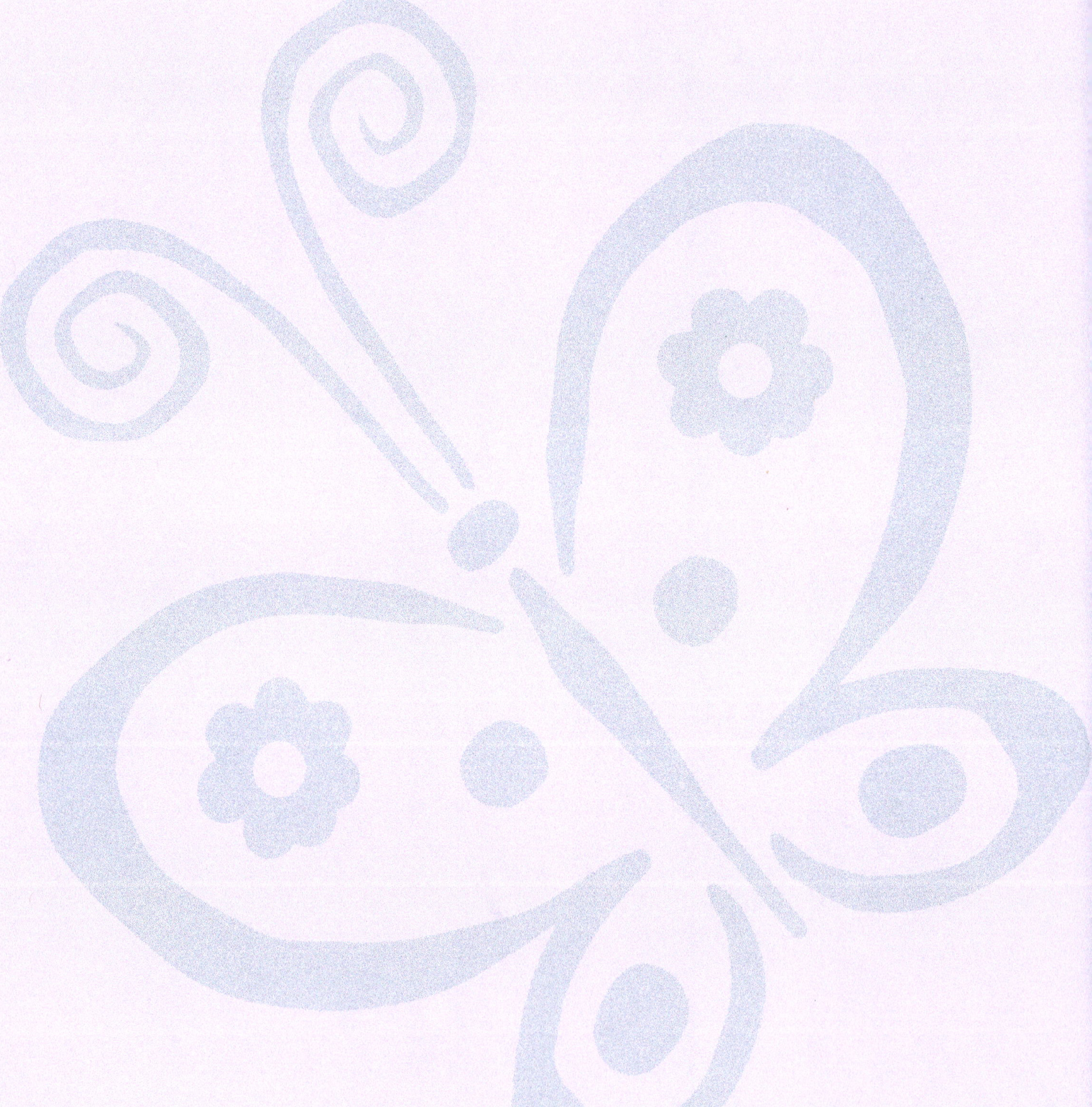

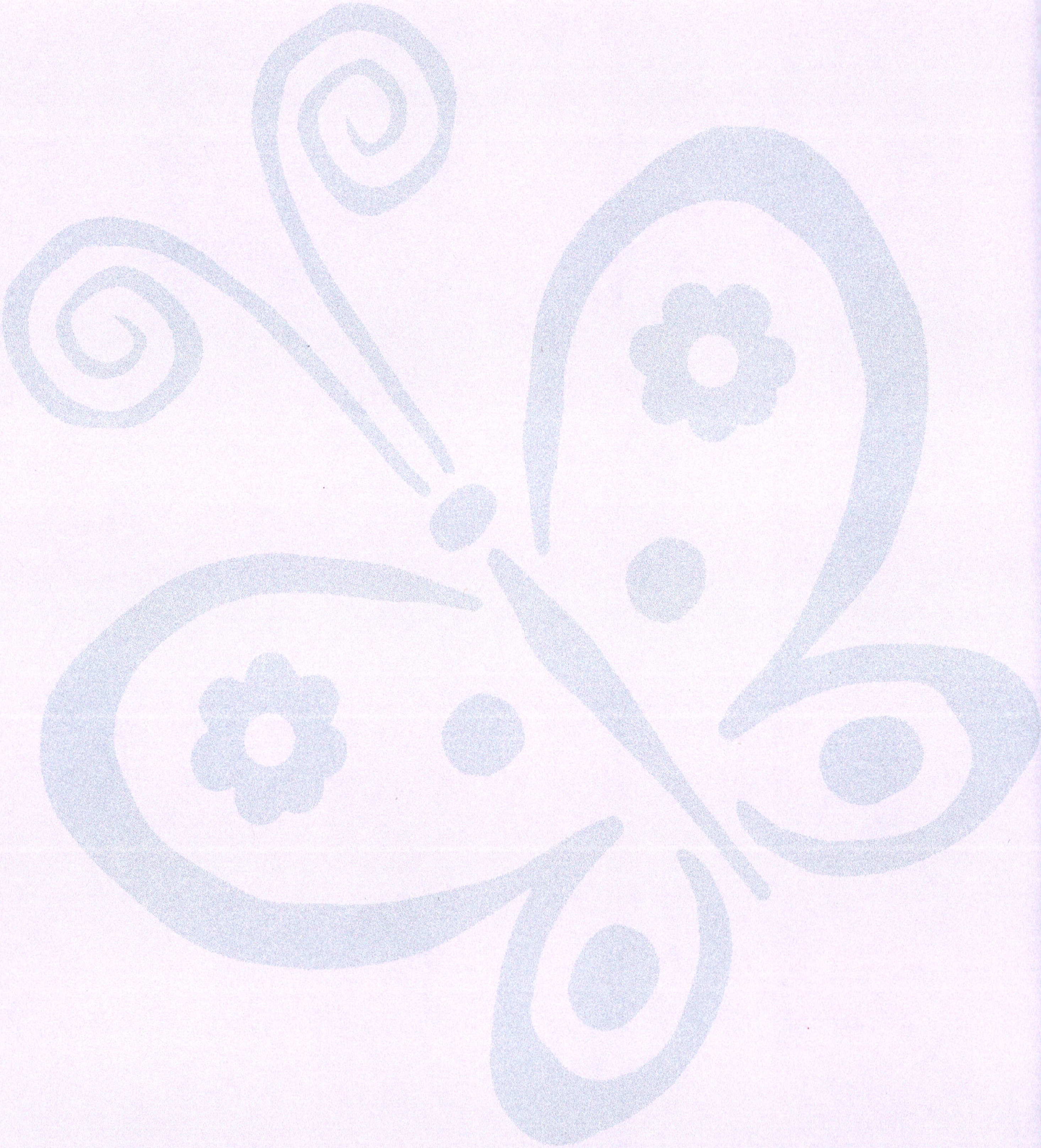

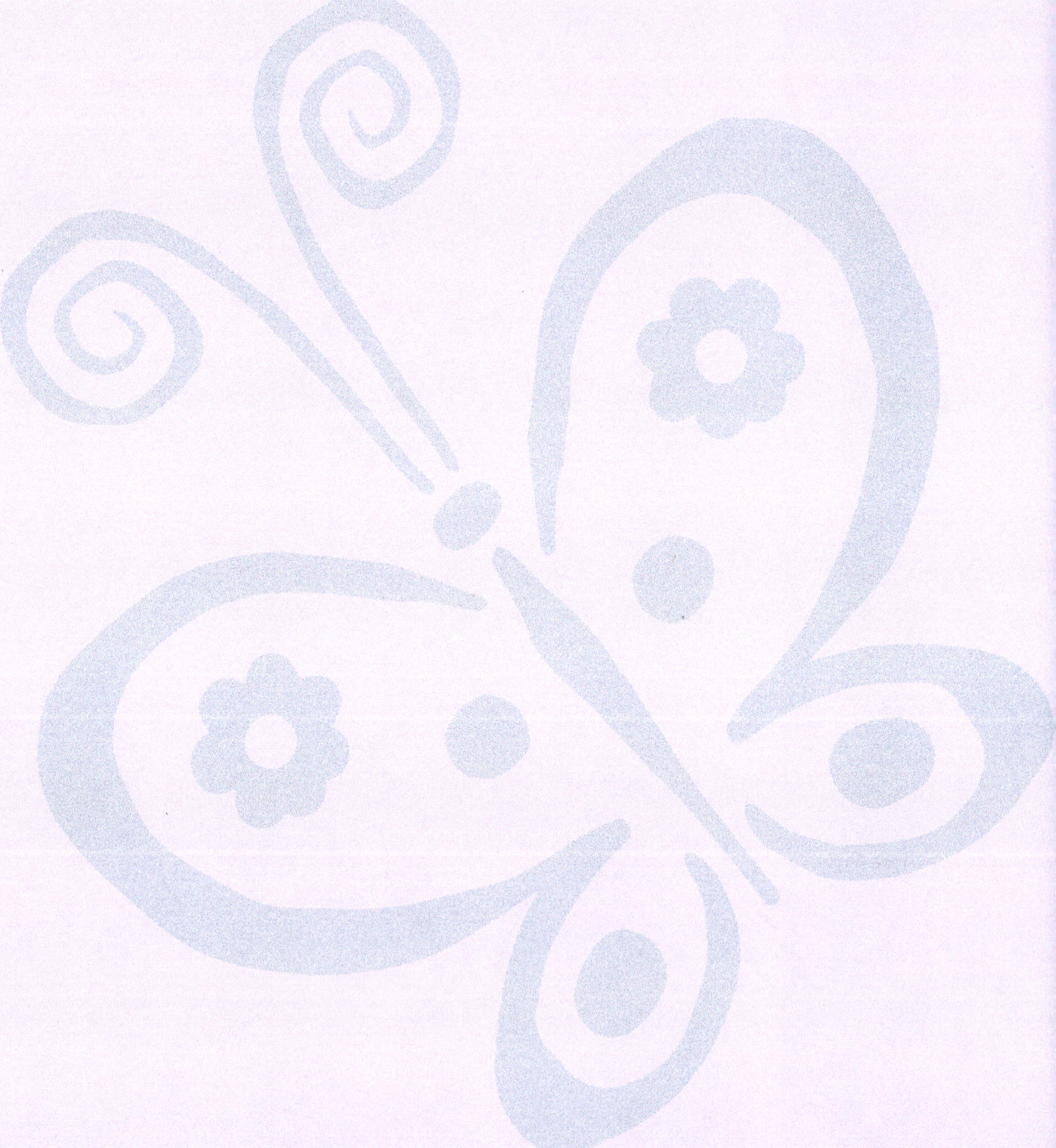

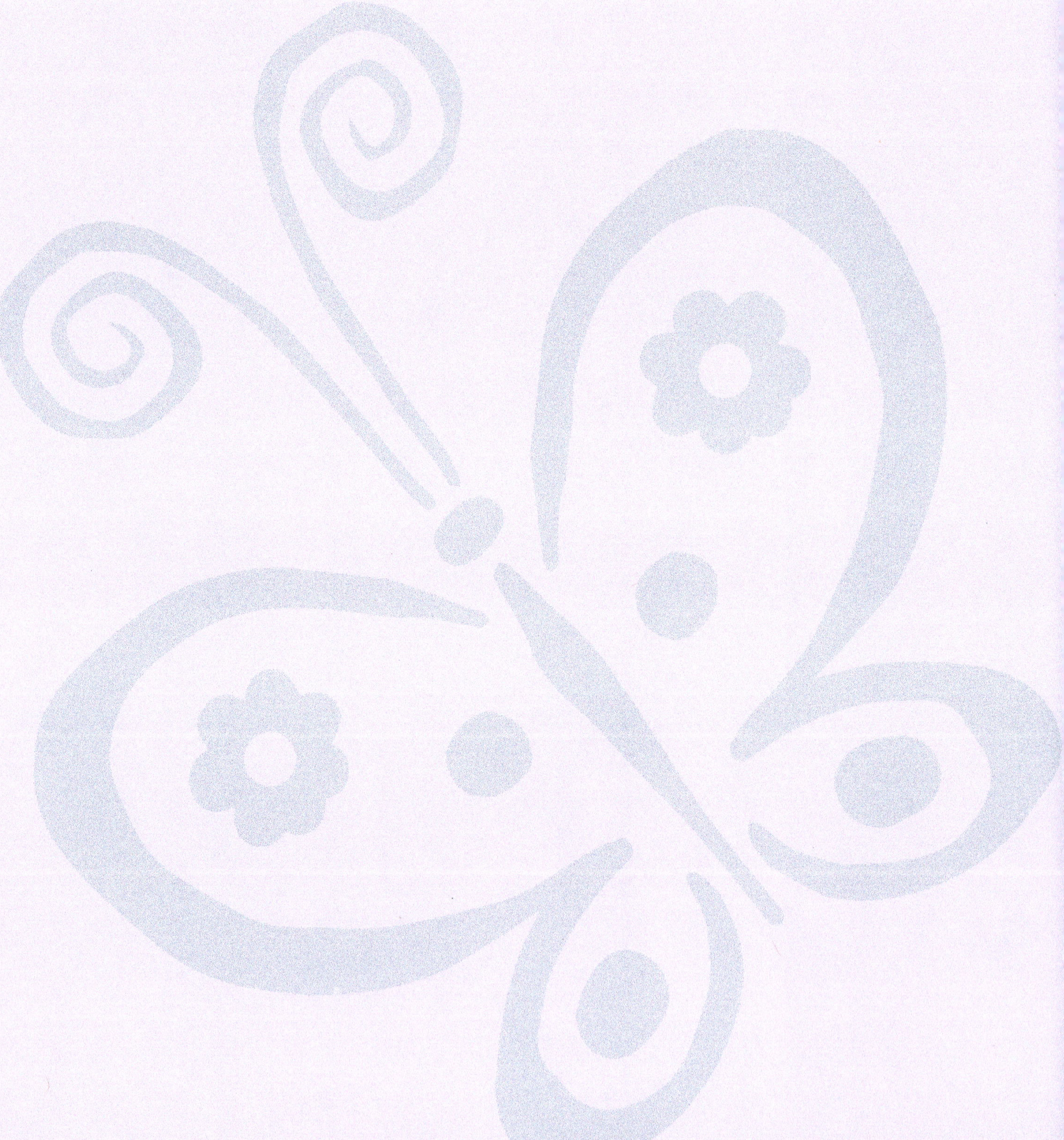

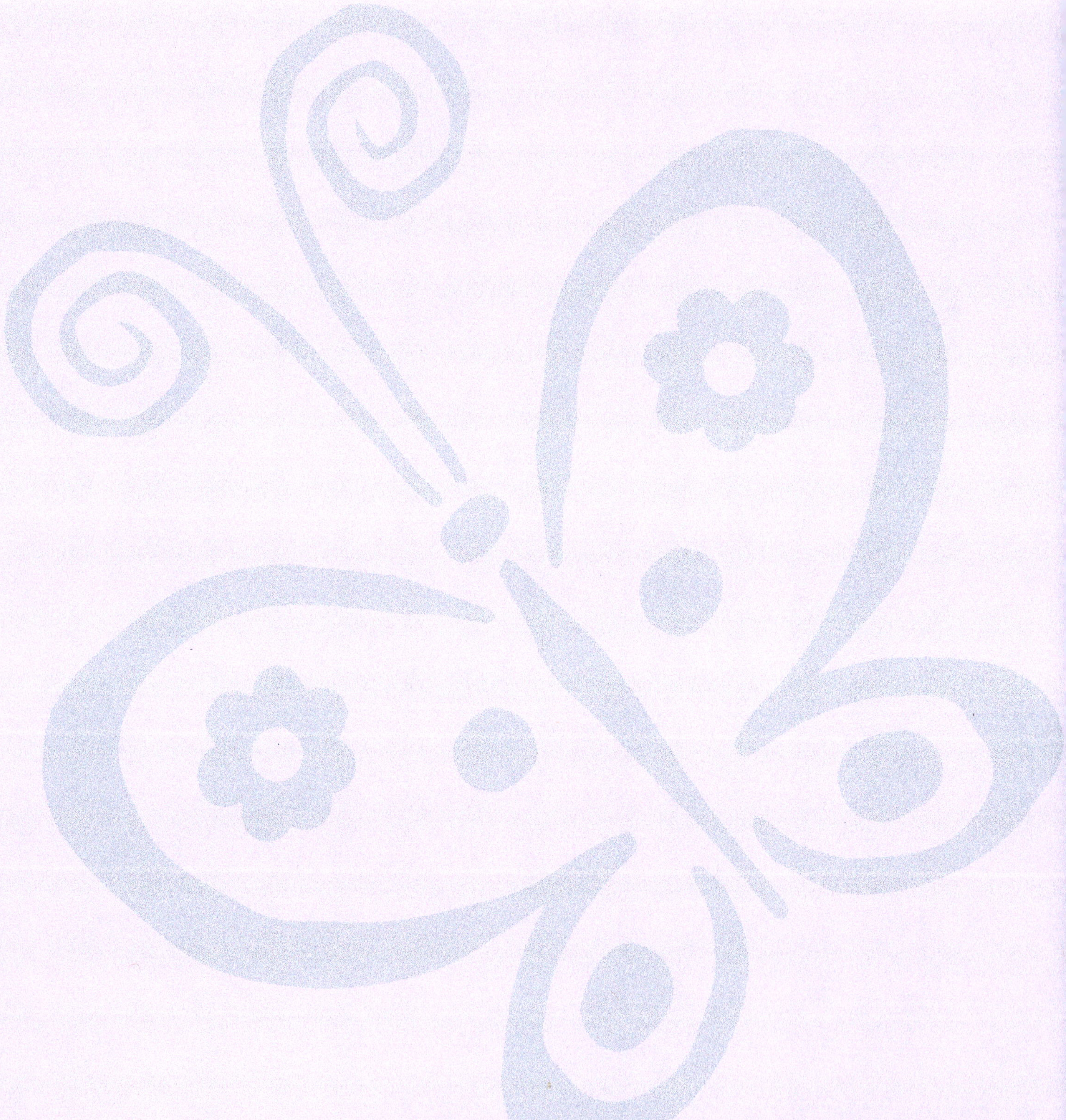

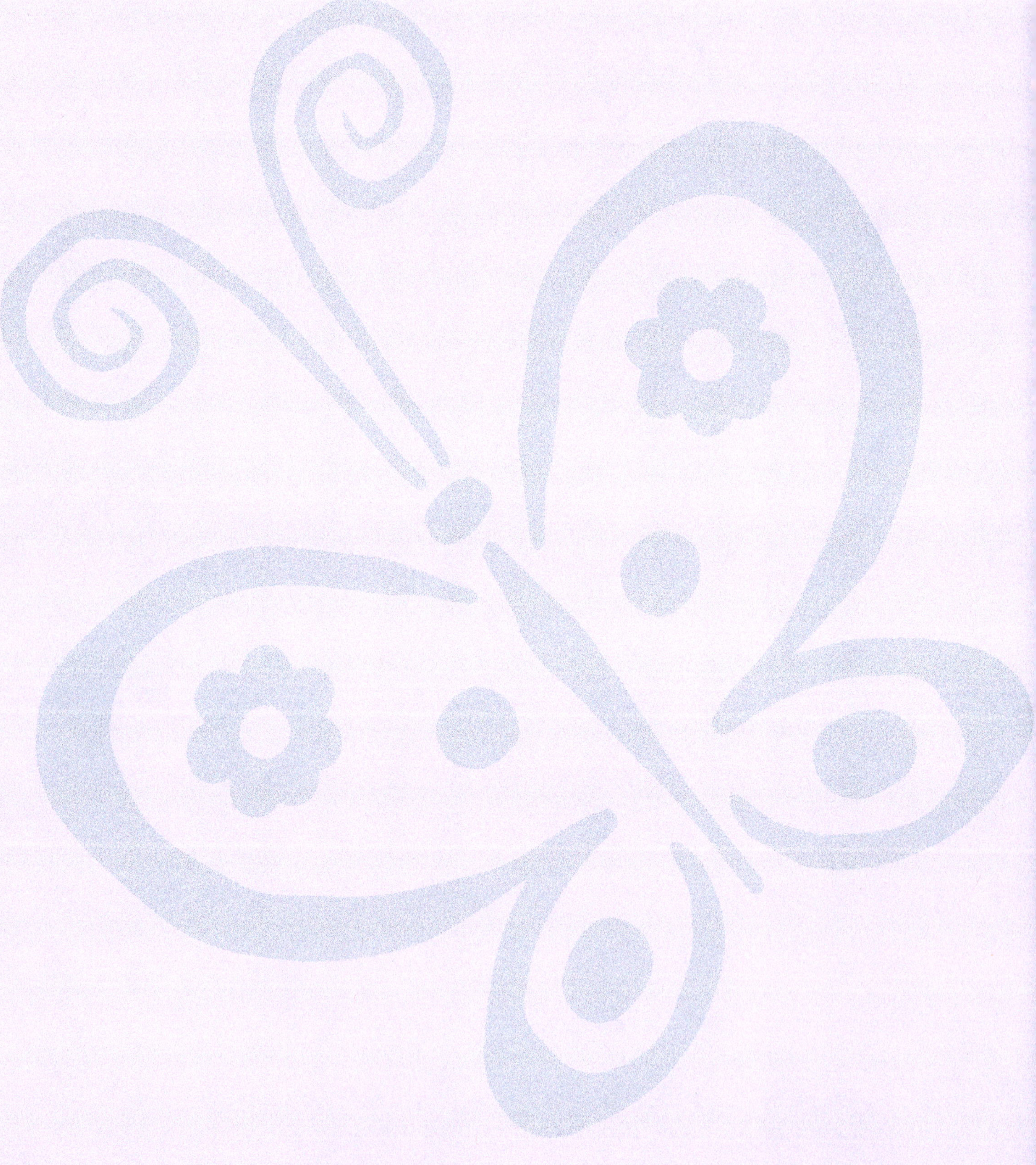

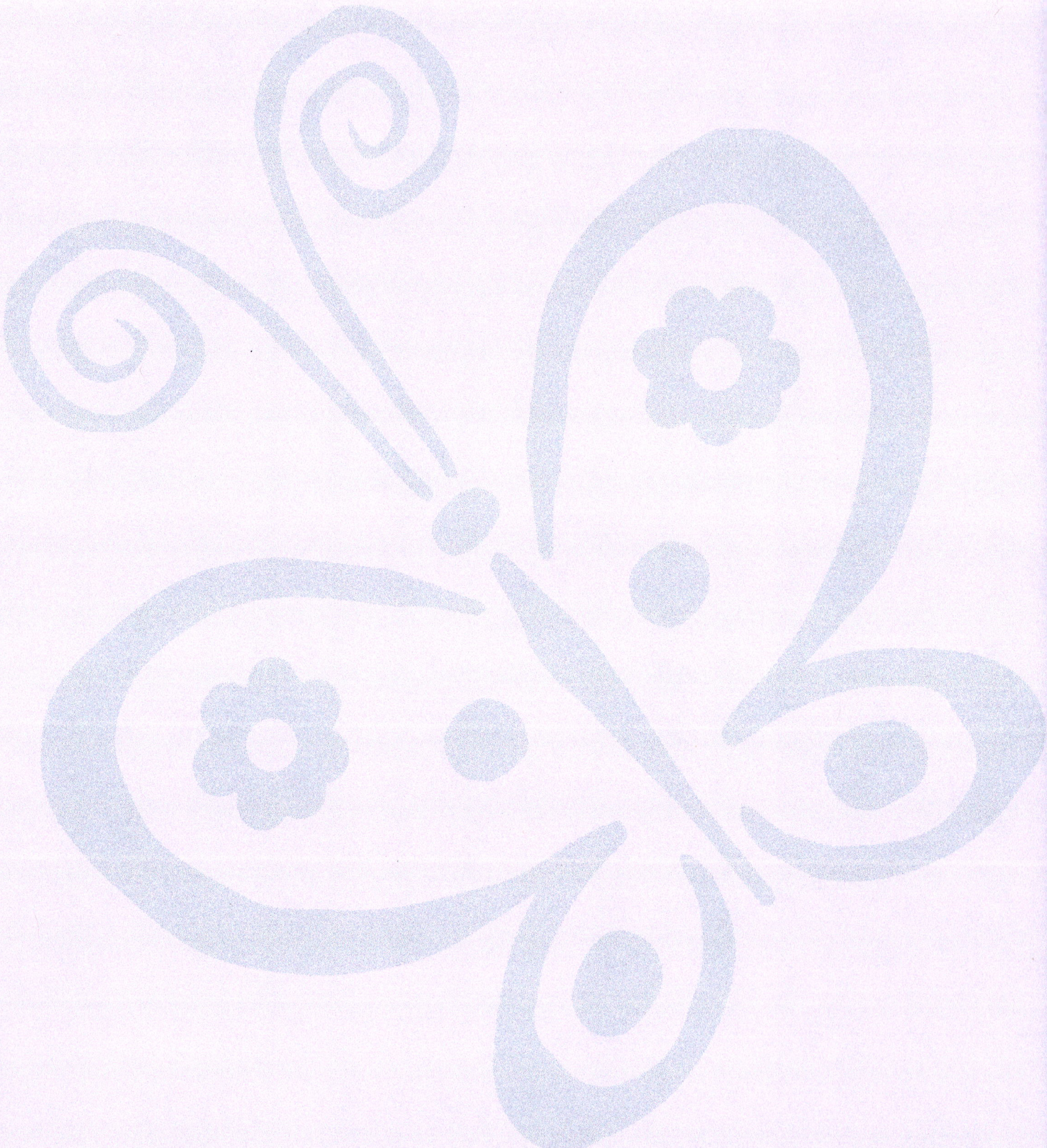

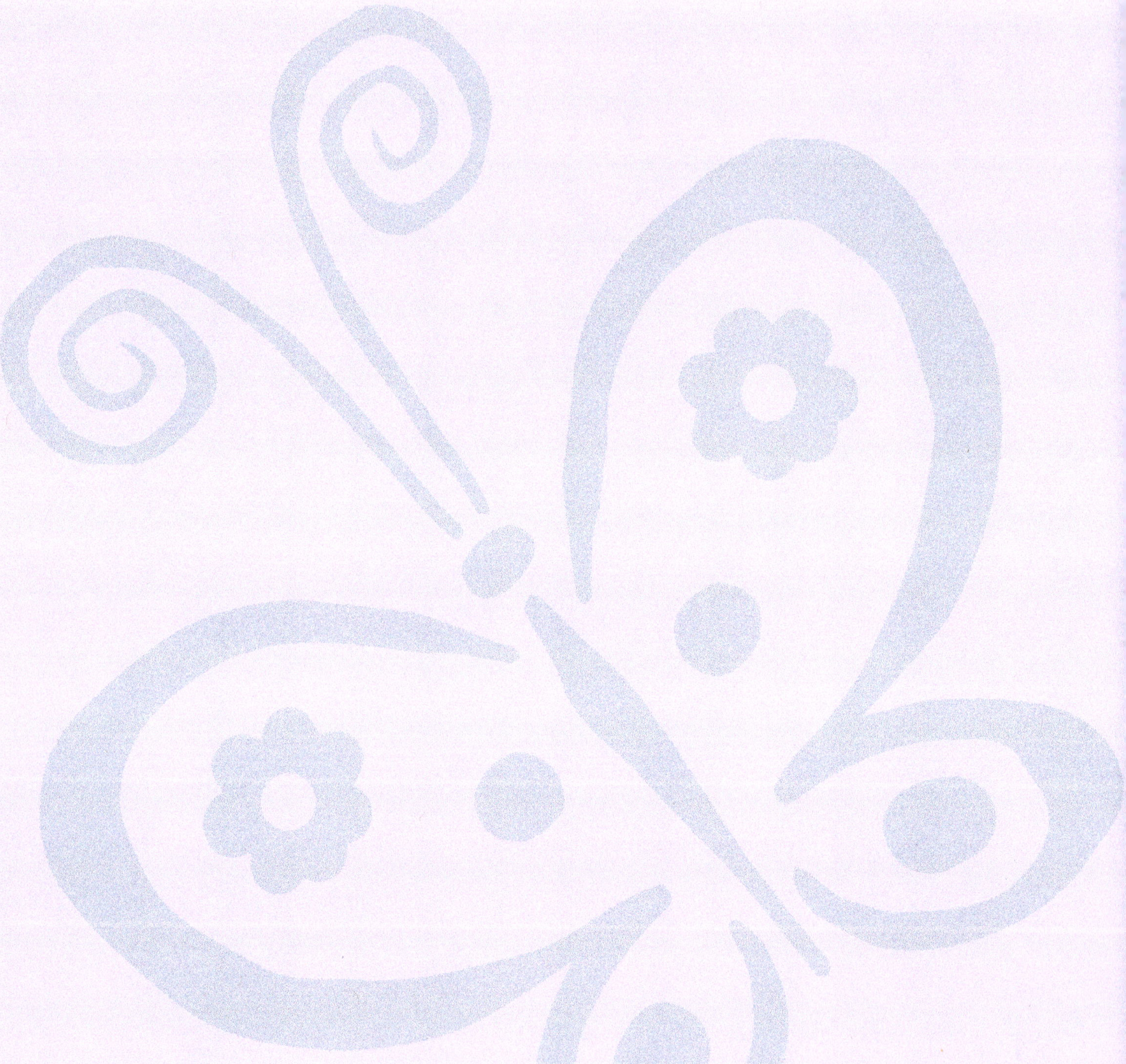

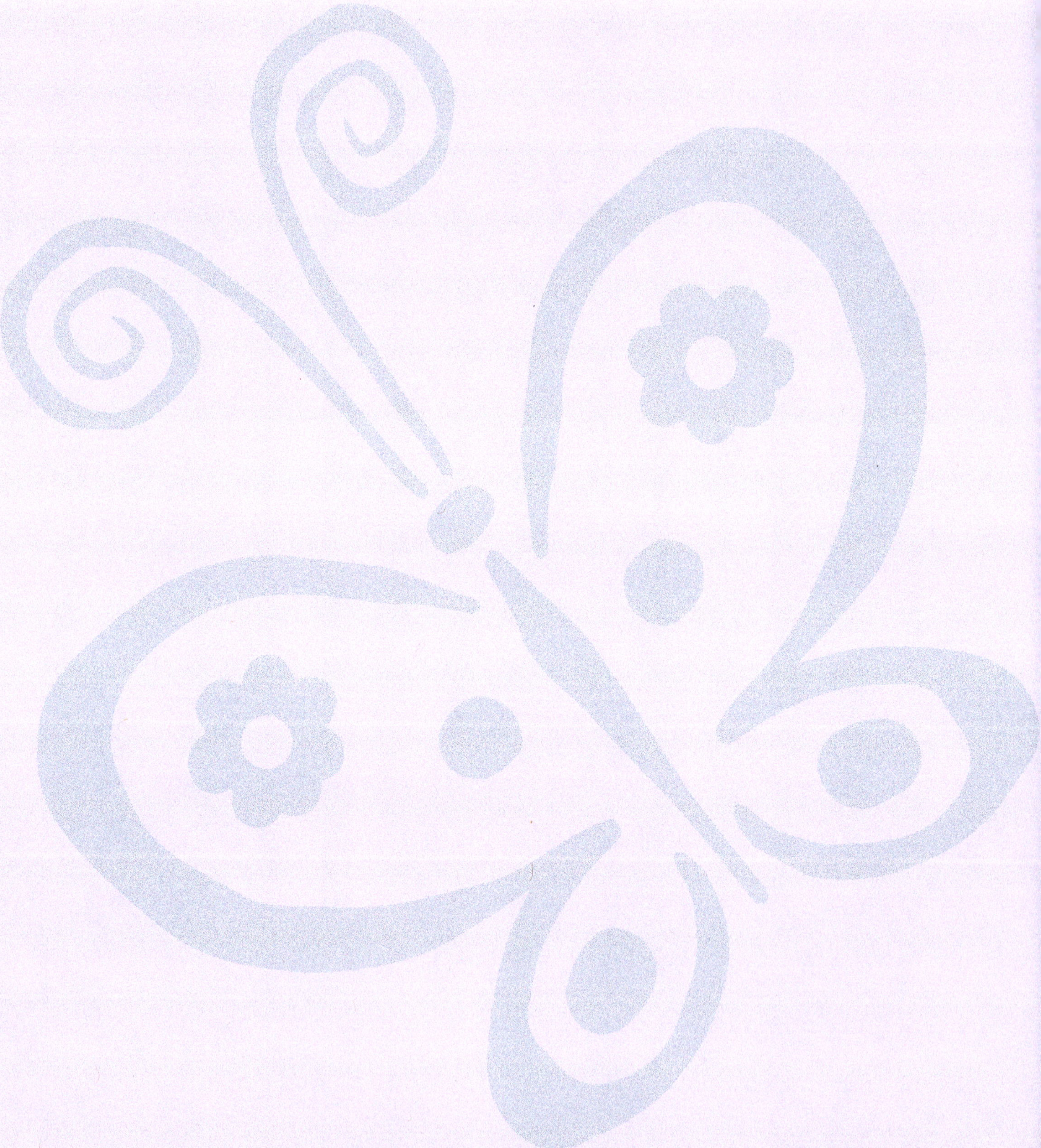

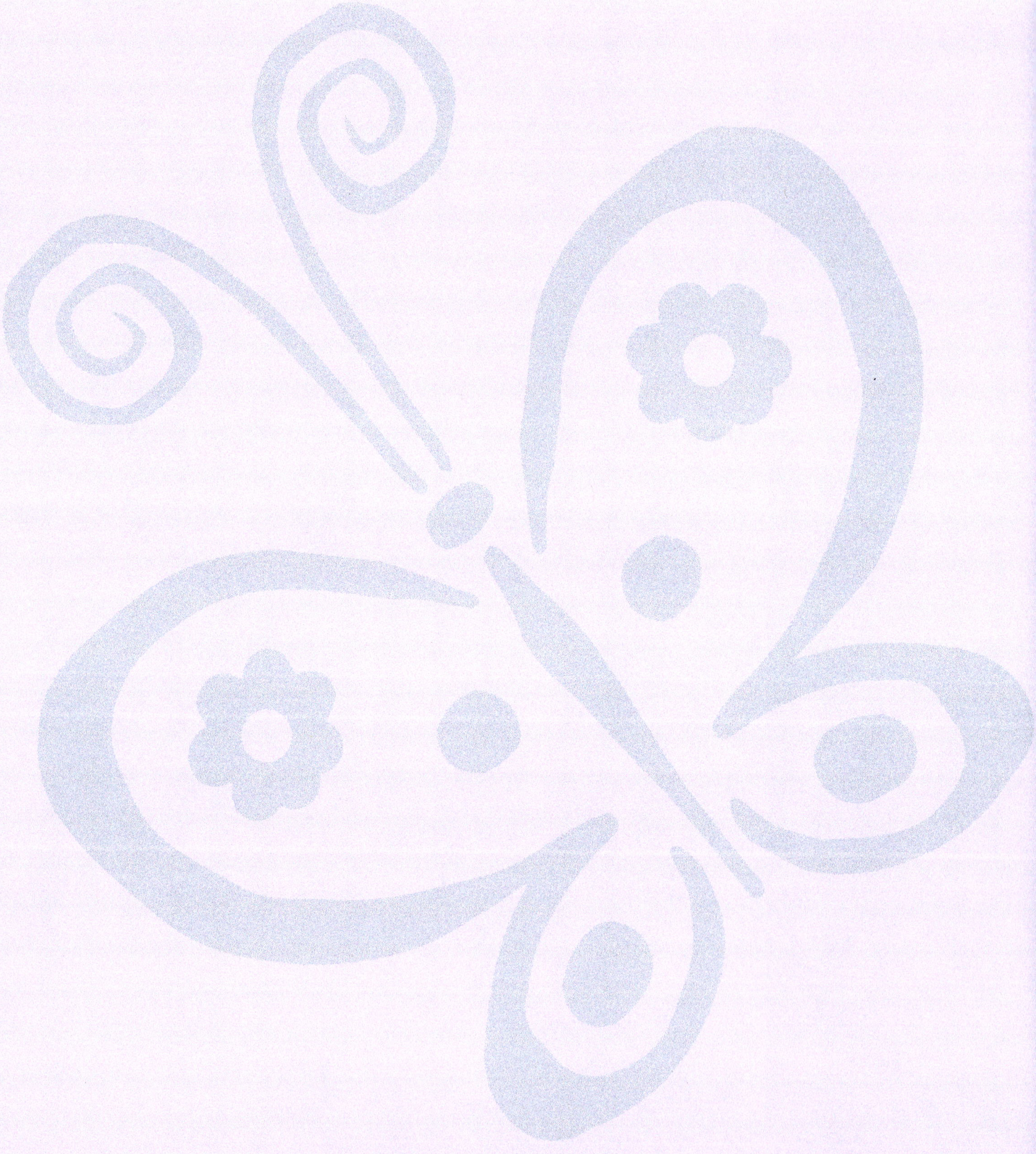

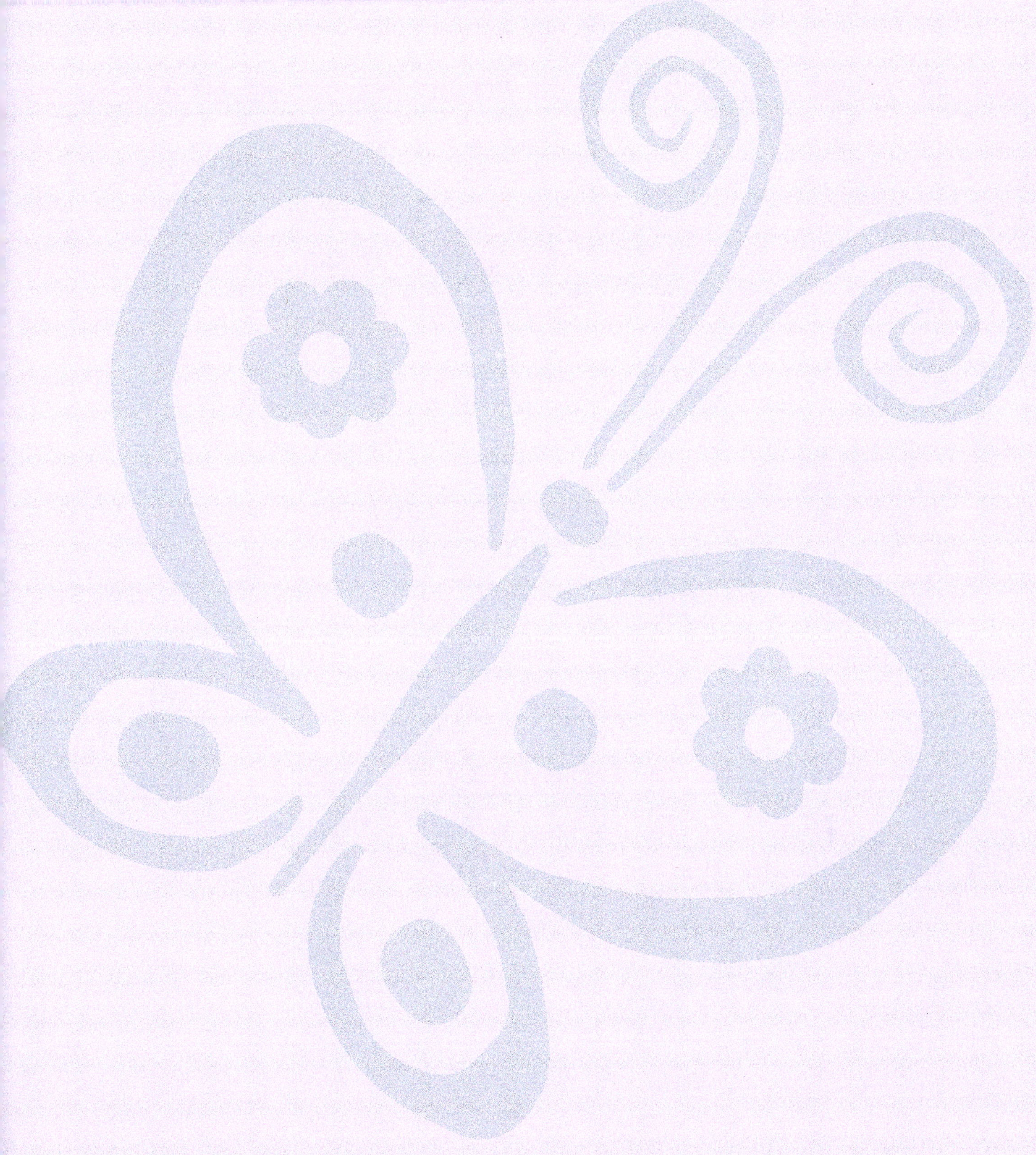

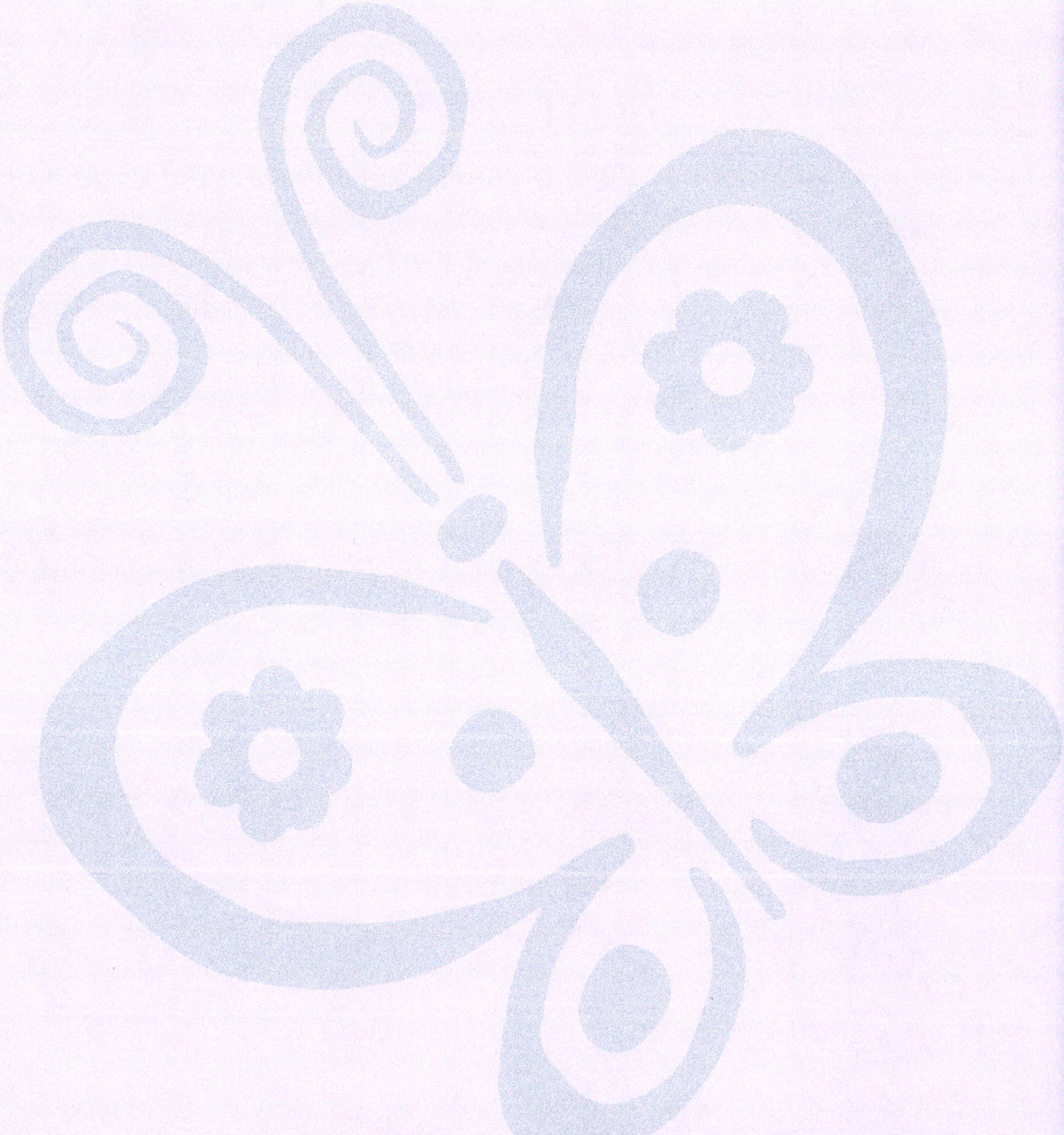

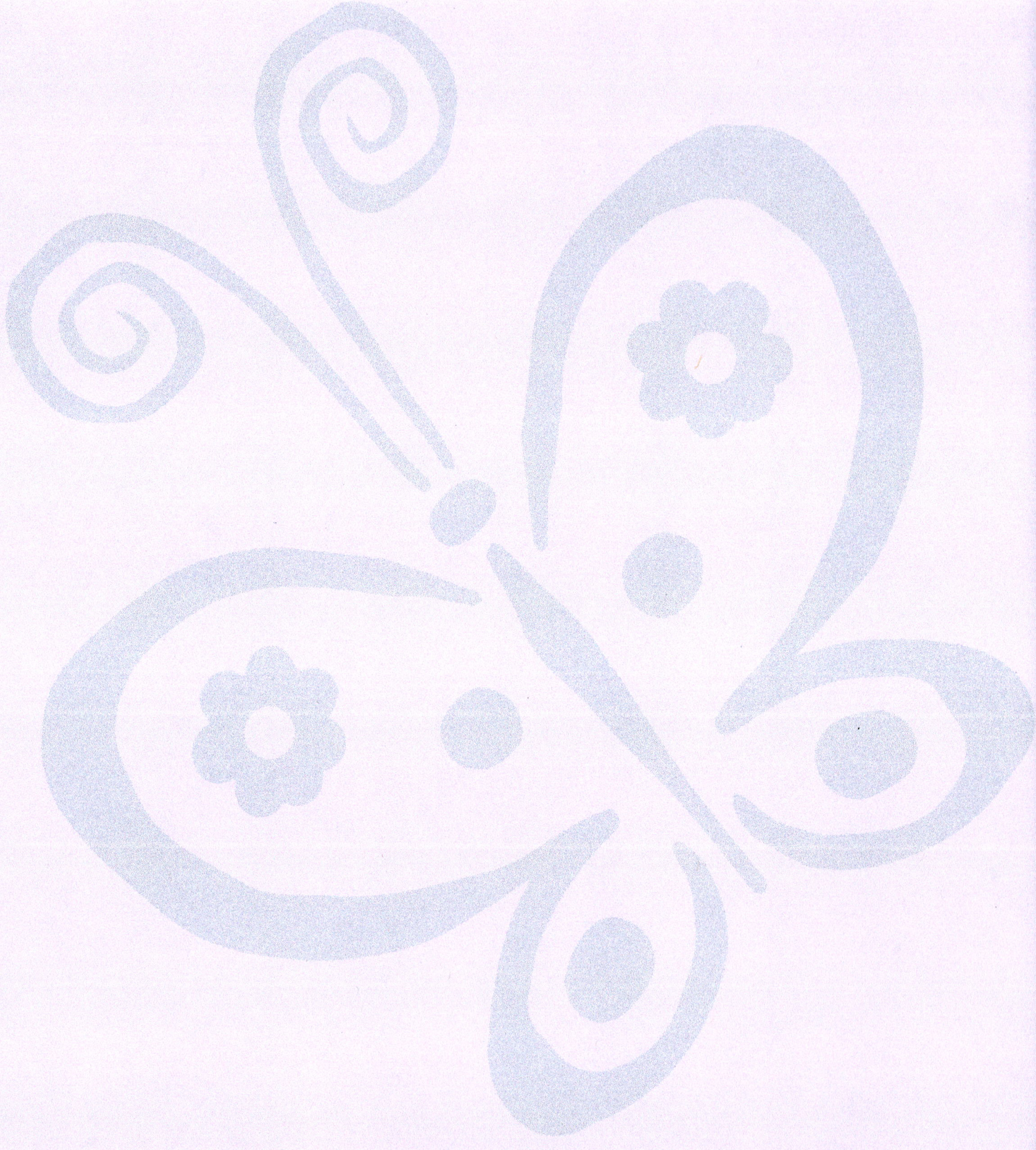

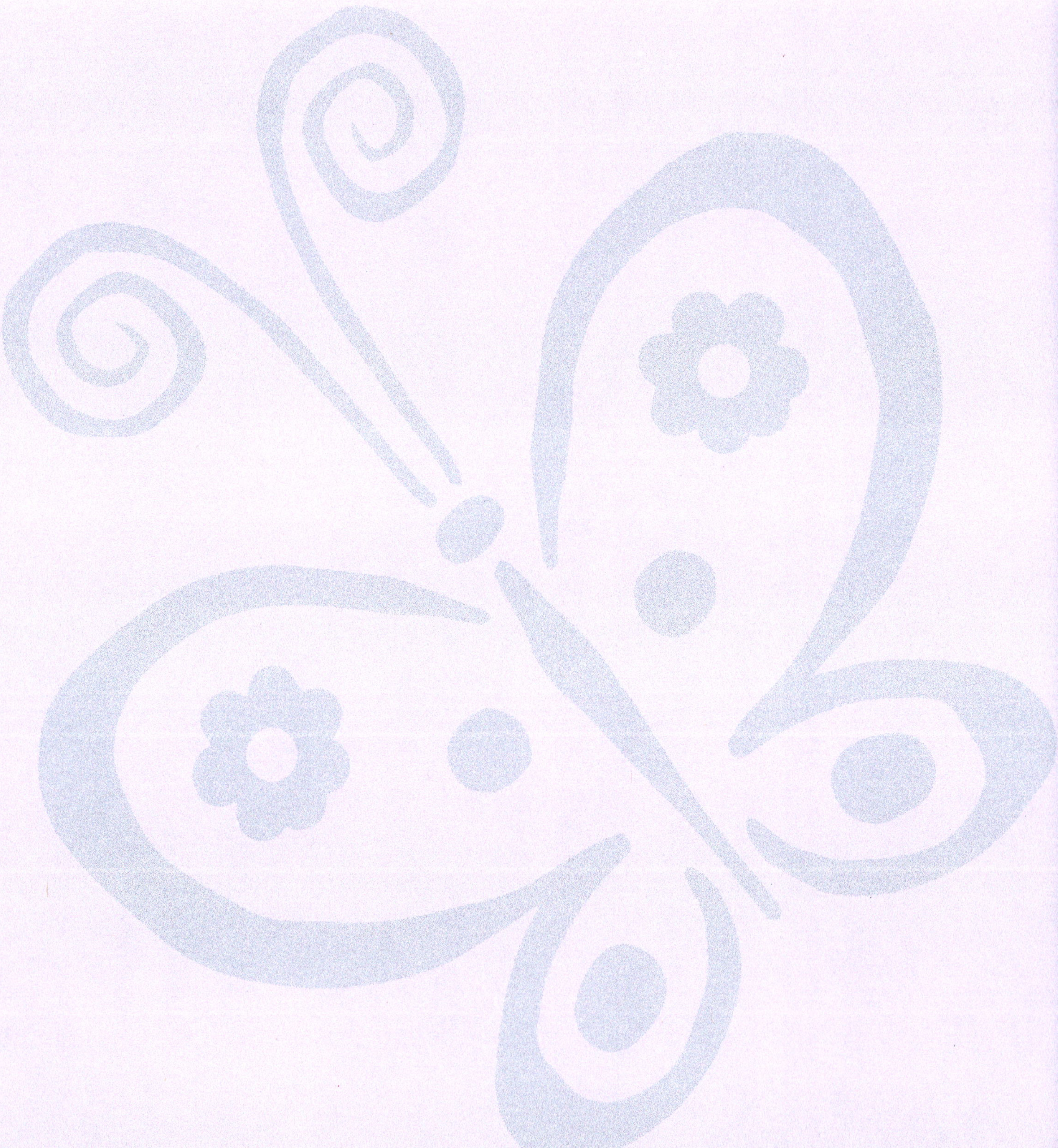

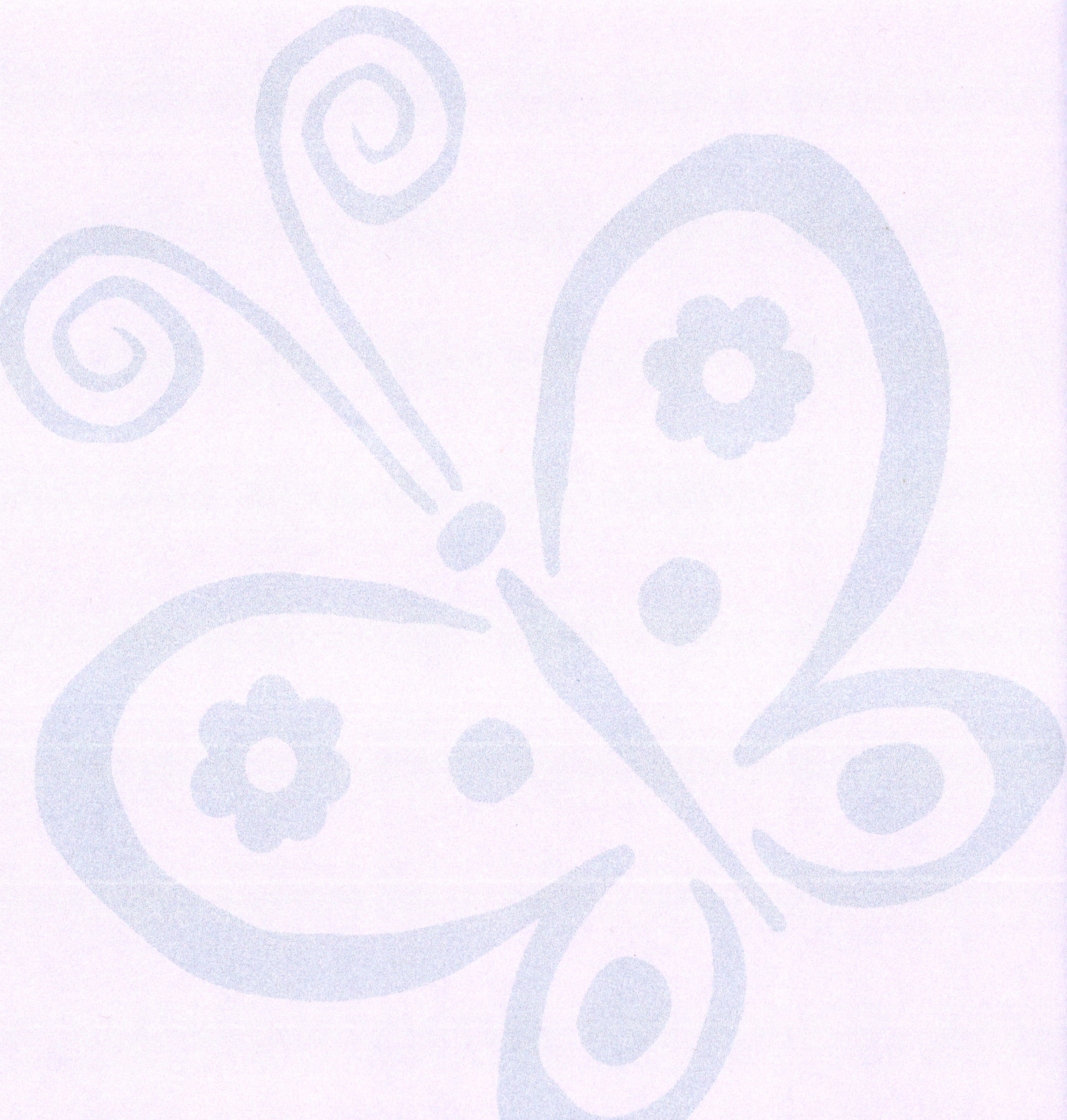

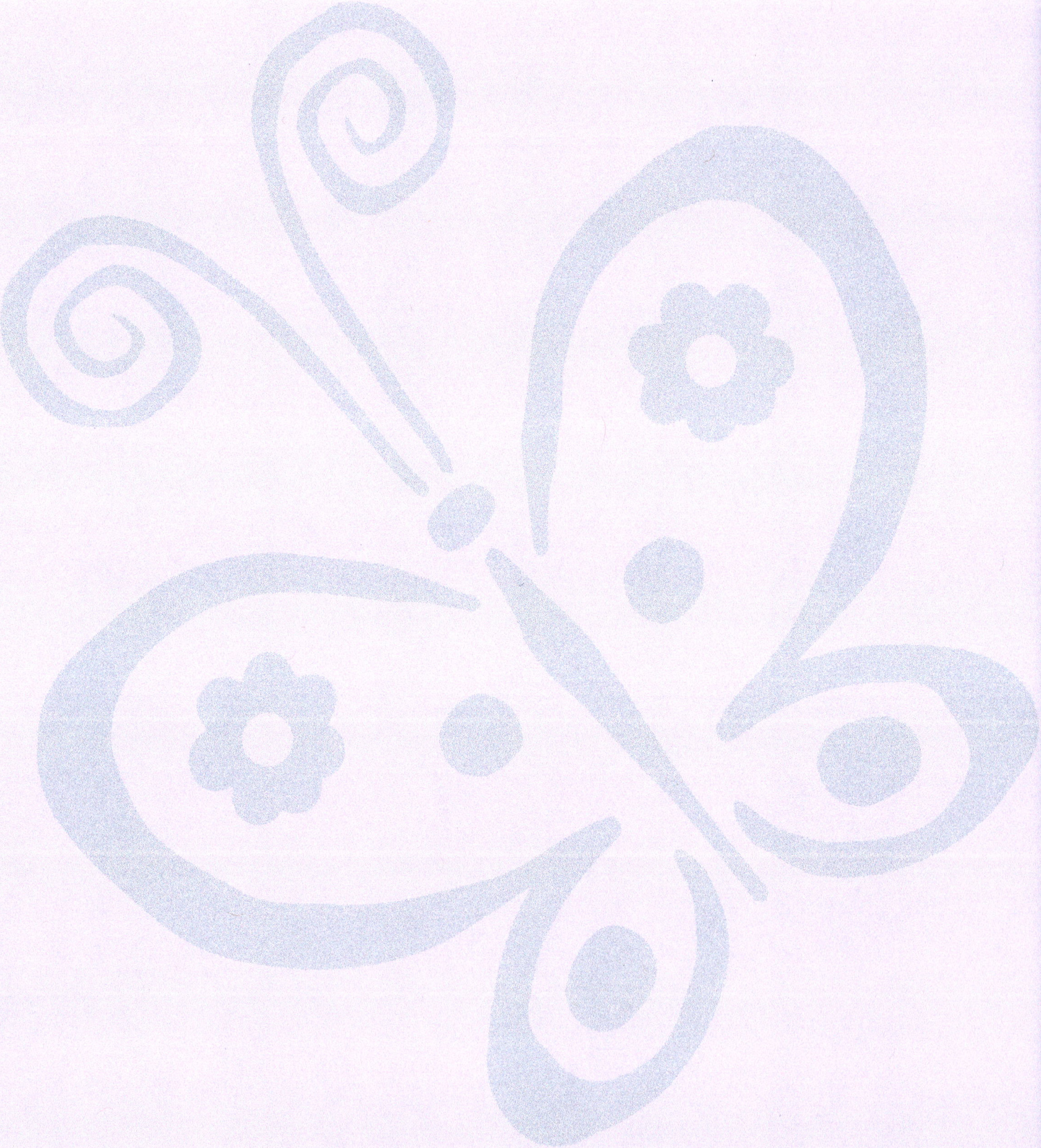

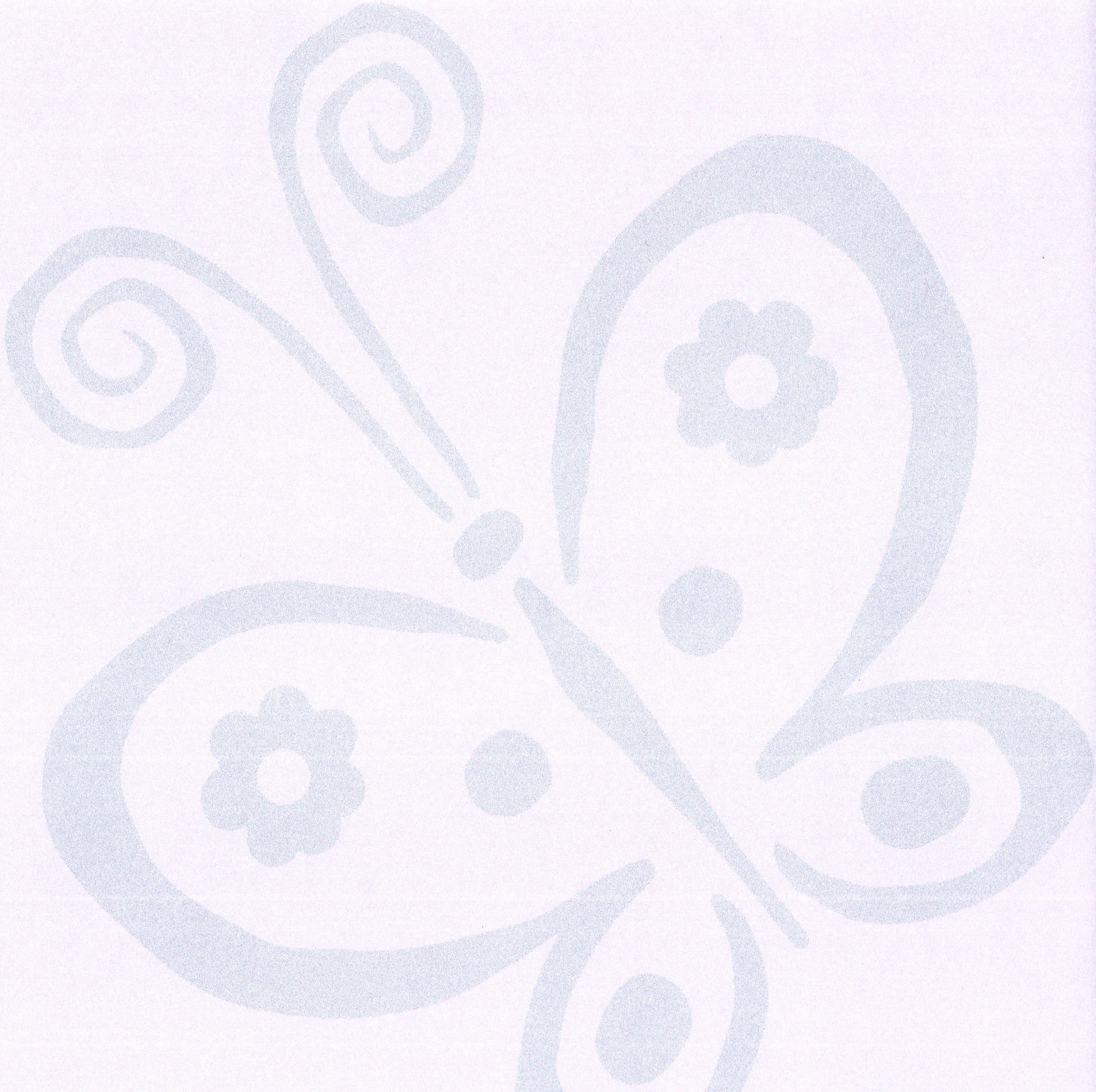

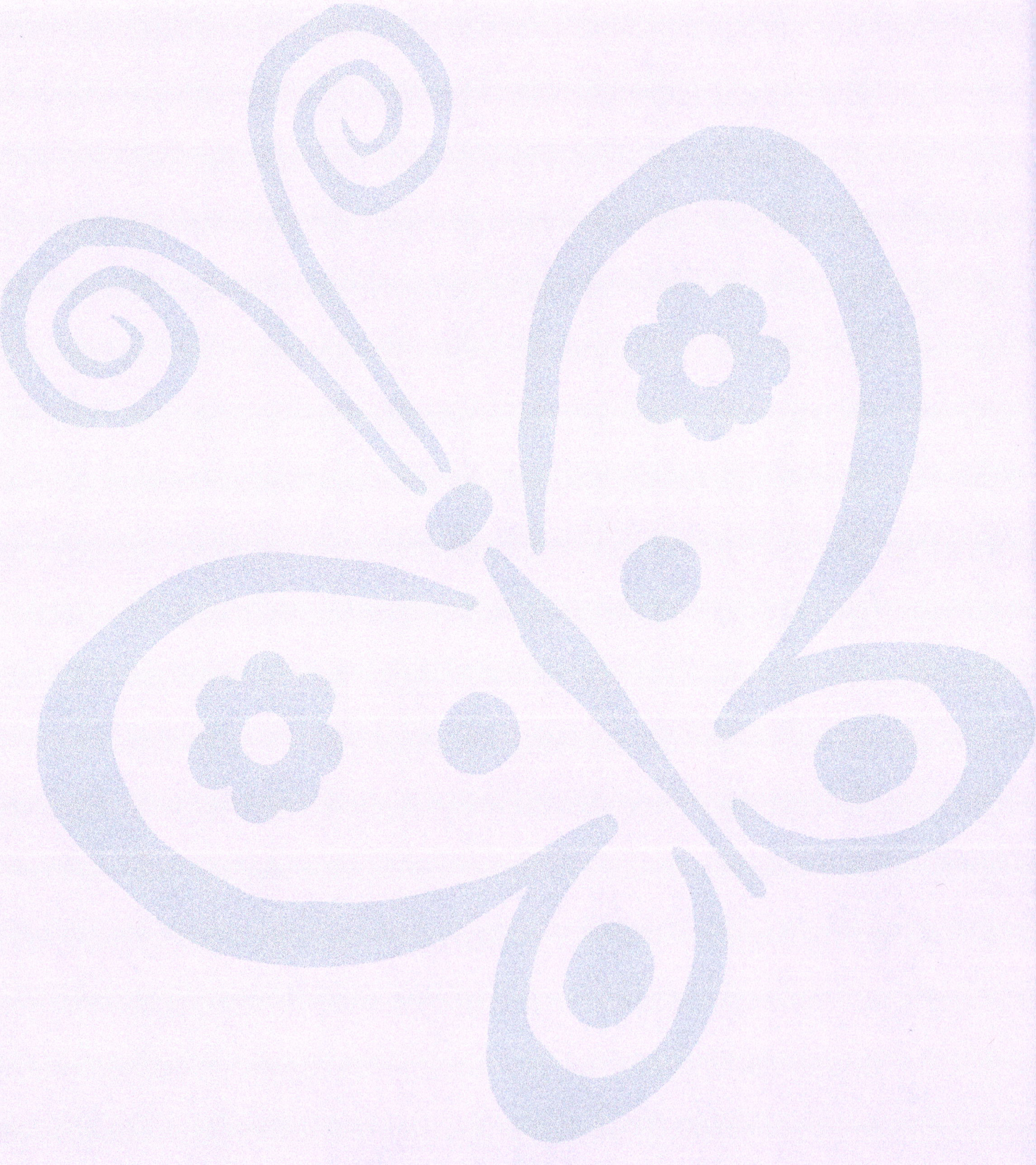

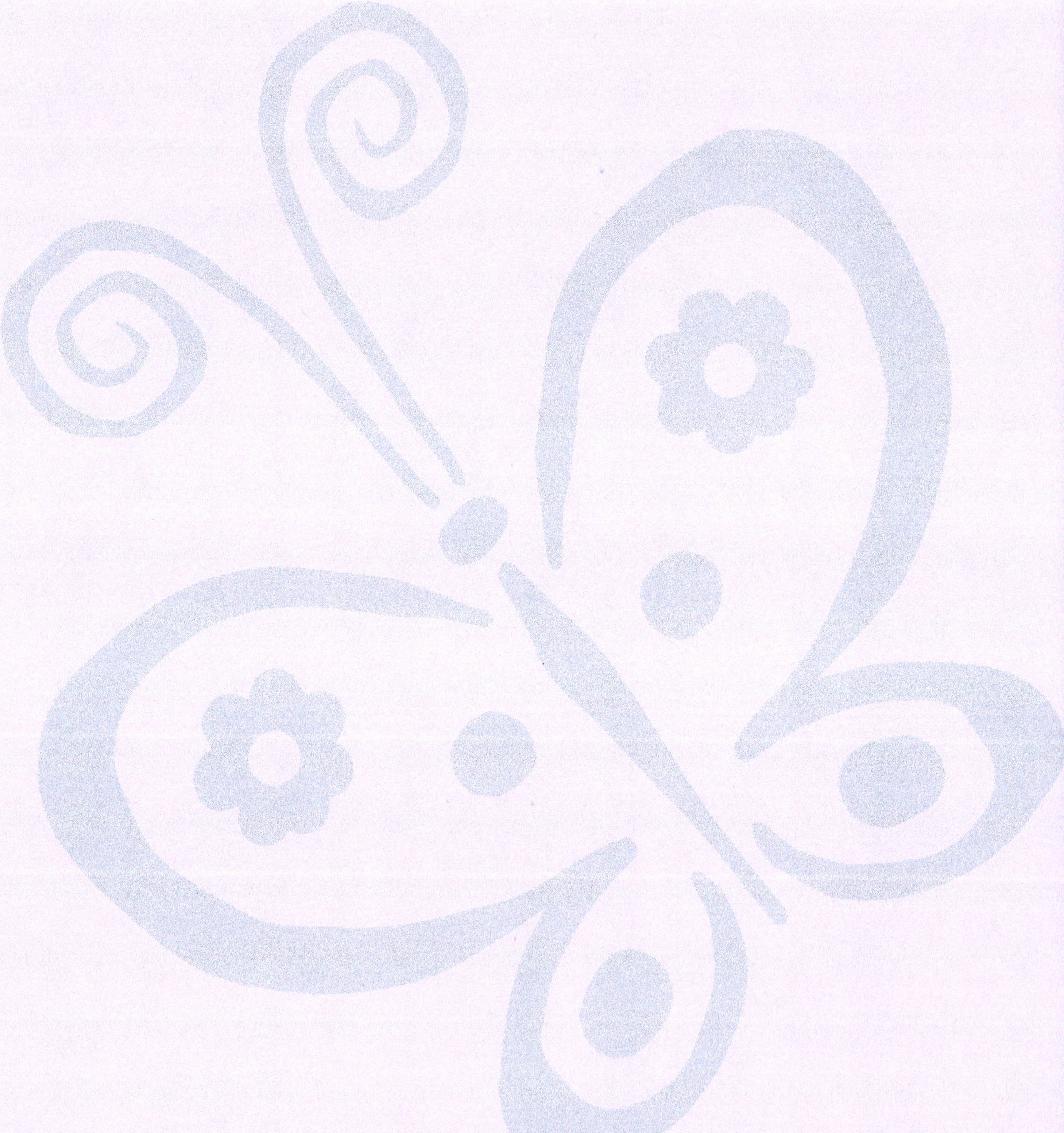

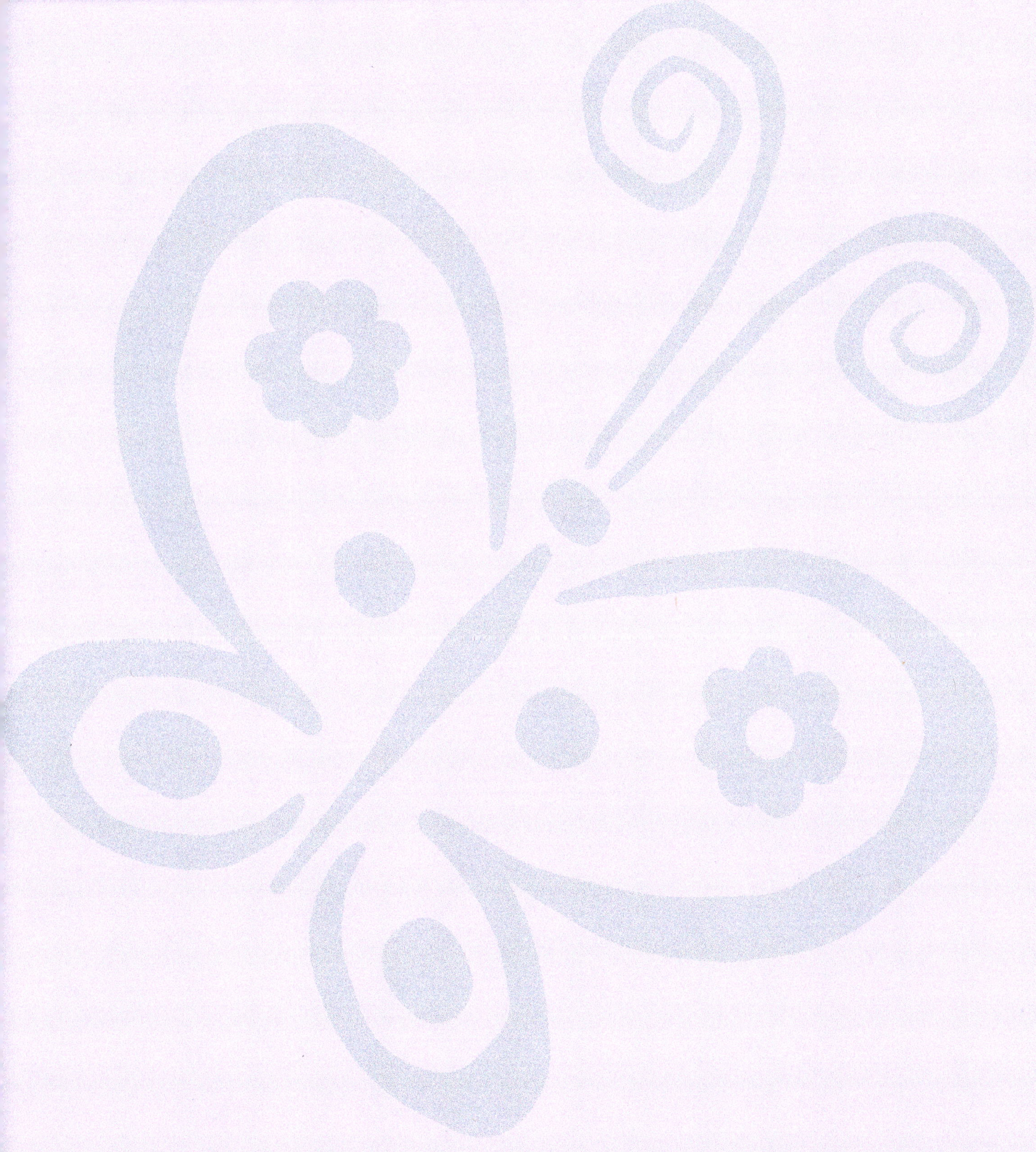

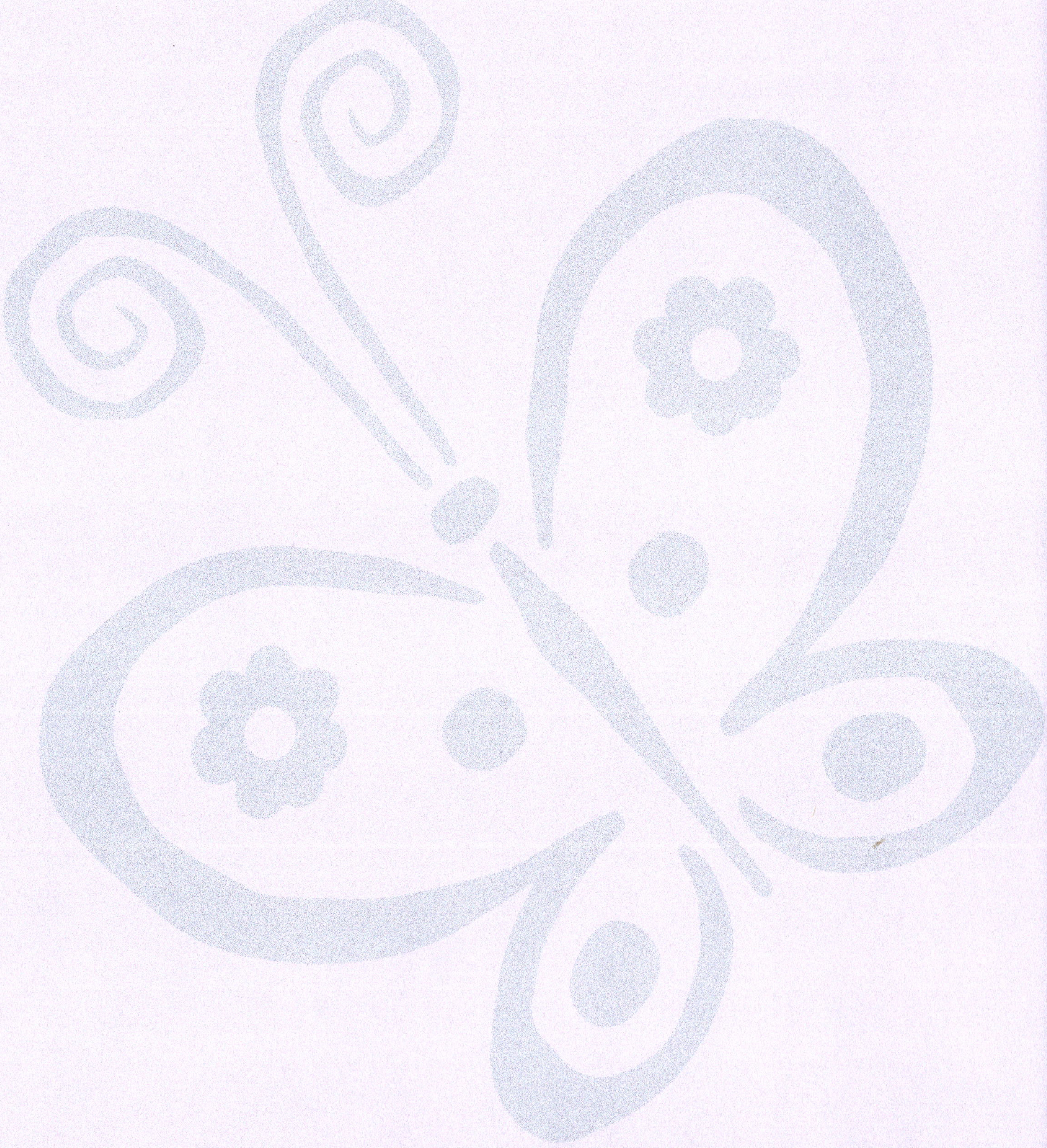

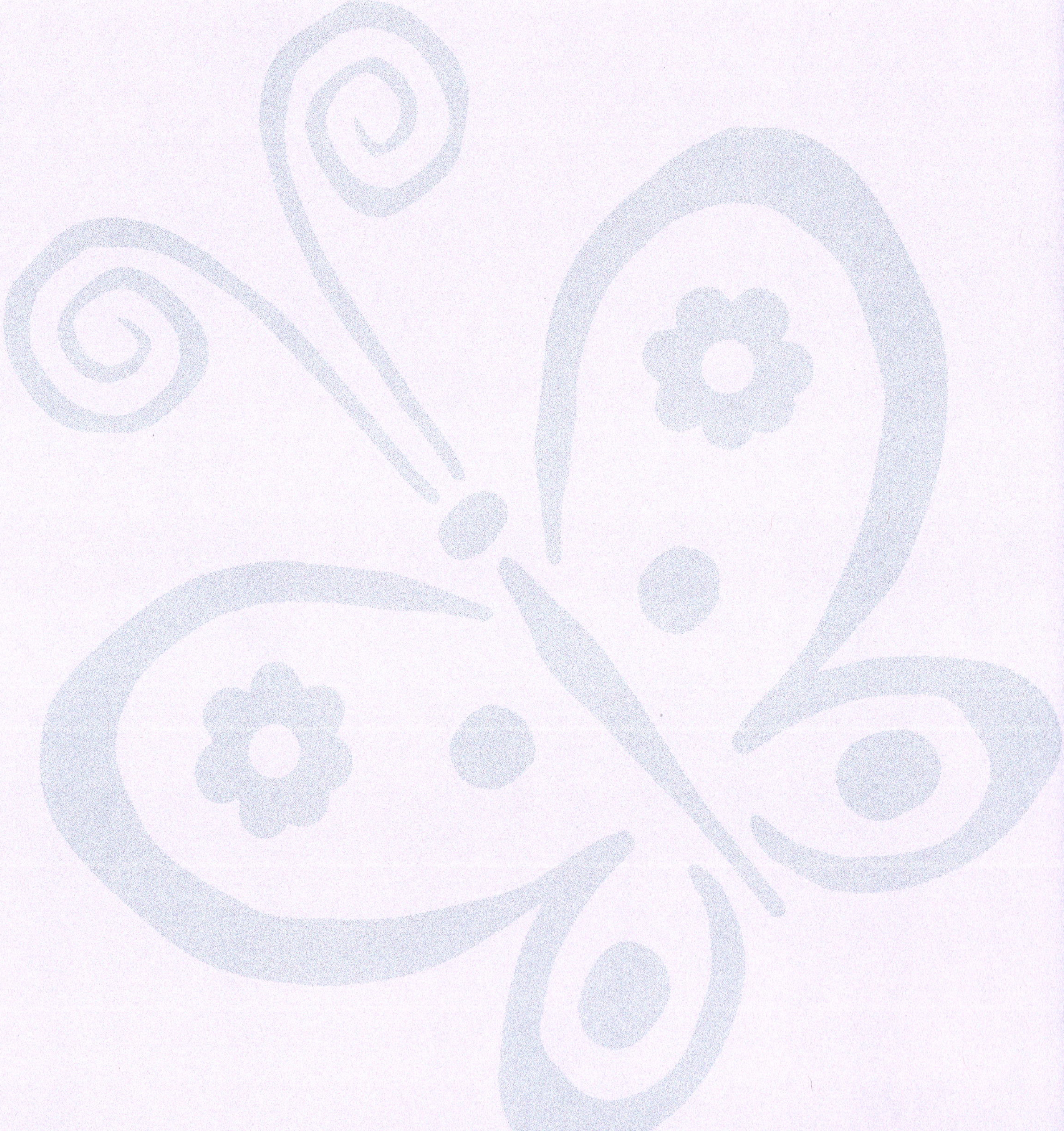